THE REAL TAX BURDEN
More than Dollars and Cents

THE REAL TAX BURDEN
More than Dollars and Cents

Alex M. Brill and Alan D. Viard

AEI Press

Publisher for the American Enterprise Institute

Washington, D.C.

Distributed by arrangement with the National Book Network
15200 NBN Way, Blue Ridge Summit, PA 17214
To order call toll free 1-800-462-6420 or 1-717-794-3800.

For all other inquiries please contact AEI Press, 1150 17th Street,
N.W., Washington, D.C. 20036 or call 1-800-862-5801.

Brill, Alex M.
   The real tax burden : more than dollars and cents / Alex M. Brill
   and Alan D. Viard.
      p. cm.
   Includes bibliographical references.
   ISBN-13: 978-0-8447-7210-3 (pbk.)
   ISBN-10: 0-8447-7210-0 (pbk.)
   ISBN-13: 978-0-8447-7211-0 (ebook)
   ISBN-10: 0-8447-7211-9 (ebook)
   1. Tax incidence—United States. 2. Externalities (Economics)
   3. Social choice. 4. Taxation—United States.
   5. Fiscal polic—United States. I. Viard, Alan D. II. Title.
   HJ2322.A3B75 2011
   33632.940973—dc23

CONTENTS

LIST OF ILLUSTRATIONS   viii

ACKNOWLEDGMENTS   ix

INTRODUCTION   1

1.   WHAT IS EXCESS BURDEN?   3

    Excess Burden of a Soda Tax   4

    Behavioral Sensitivity and Excess Burden   10

    Tax Rate and Excess Burden   13

    Excess Burden of Subsidies   15

    Other Issues in Excess Burden   18

    Summary   20

    Appendix: Graphing Excess Burden with
       Supply-and-Demand Curves   21

2.   EXCESS BURDEN OF WAGE, INCOME, AND
    CONSUMPTION TAXES   23

    Wage, Income, and Consumption Taxes
       in a No-Saving World   24

    The Income Tax Penalizes Saving   28

    Wage and Consumption Taxes Do Not
       Penalize Saving   30

    Saving and Economic Growth   32

    Summary   34

3. TAXATION IN THE UNITED STATES: AN OVERVIEW   35
    Individual Income Tax   38
    Payroll Taxes   46
    Corporate Income Tax   47
    Excise, Estate, and Gift Taxes   49
    U.S. Tax System versus Other Countries   50
    Summary   51

4. ISSUES IN U.S. PERSONAL INCOME TAXATION   53
    Understanding Tax Expenditures   55
    Standard Deduction and Personal Exemption   57
    Top Tax Expenditures   58
    Marginal and Average Tax Rates   66
    Phase-Outs and Effective Marginal Tax Rates   69
    The Big Picture: The Sensitivity of Taxable
        Income to Tax Rates   70
    Shrinking Income Tax Rolls   70
    Summary   71

5. ISSUES IN U.S. BUSINESS TAXATION   73
    Structural Components of Business Taxation   74
    Corporate Income Tax Rates   75
    Asset Depreciation   76
    Debt versus Equity Financing   77
    International Issues   78

Sector-Specific Issues   80
Pass-Through Entities   81
Corporate Income Tax Controversy   82
Summary   82

6. OPTIONS FOR FUNDAMENTAL TAX REFORM   85
    Different Ways to Tax Consumption   86
    Comparison of Consumption Taxes   90
    Summary   93

CONCLUSION   95
SUGGESTED READING   97
ABOUT THE AUTHORS   101

LIST OF ILLUSTRATIONS

FIGURE

1   Four Ways to Tax Consumption   88

TABLES

1   Historical Trends in Federal Revenue Sources   37
2   2011 Individual Income Tax Rates   41
3   Individual Tax Expenditures by Budget
     Function, 2010   59
4   Top Ten Individual Tax Expenditures, 2010   60

ACKNOWLEDGMENTS

The authors thank Meagan Berry, Earl Grinols, Chad Hill, Henry Olsen, Christy Robinson, Eric Teetsel, and Andy Yuengert for helpful comments.

INTRODUCTION

When people discuss taxes, it is often to complain about them. In these discussions, the tax burden one faces is almost always assumed to be the dollars and cents paid to the government. This limited focus on tax payments threatens to obscure what many economists consider the real tax burden, which they refer to as the excess burden of taxation.

Although tax payments are burdensome to taxpayers, they provide revenue to the government, which can use them to provide benefits and services that offset the burden (if the benefits and services are provided effectively and lie within government's legitimate role). In contrast, the excess burden discussed in this book is pure waste that provides no revenue to the government. As we explain in the upcoming pages, excess burden arises when taxes interfere with the taxpayer's freedom to choose his or her preferred behavior. This interference with freedom is the real tax burden, more than the dollars and cents paid to the government.

1

WHAT IS EXCESS BURDEN?

This chapter provides an introduction to excess burden, the central concept of this book. As we explain, excess burden measures the extent to which a tax interferes with the taxpayer's freedom to choose his or her preferred behavior. Popular discussions of tax policy often focus on the obvious burden of taxation: the amount of taxes people pay. But excess burden arises when behavior changes in a way that causes taxes to not be paid. Excess burden is, in many ways, the real tax burden.

Our ultimate goal is to look at the excess burden of the actual U.S. tax system and how the tax system can be changed to reduce excess burden. We approach this topic in stages. We begin in this chapter by considering the excess burden of a simple hypothetical tax, a tax on soda. In chapter 2, we explain the kinds of excess burden that generally arise from wage, income, and consumption taxes. In chapters 3 through 5, we apply this analysis to the wage and income taxes actually imposed by the federal government and discuss improvements that could be made within those tax systems. In chapter 6, we discuss a more fundamental reform, the partial or complete replacement of income taxation by consumption taxation, which could further reduce excess burden by ending tax penalties on saving.

EXCESS BURDEN OF A SODA TAX

Although we use a soda tax as our initial example, the type of product is not important. The same principles apply to a tax on any other product, or, as we will discuss in chapter 2, to wage, income, and consumption taxes.

Suppose that producers can supply an unlimited amount of soda at a cost of $10 per carton, where the cost includes the minimum profit sufficient to attract capital to the soda industry. Assuming competitive markets, each carton of soda is sold to consumers for $10, in the absence of any taxes on soda. Suppose that, at this price, 100 cartons of soda are produced and sold.

The production of these 100 cartons is mutually beneficial to consumers and producers. (We assume that the production of soda does not cause pollution or otherwise affect third parties.) Producers—workers, owners of capital, and others involved in the production process—are willing to produce each of these cartons in exchange for a $10 payment. Consumers place a value of at least $10 on each carton, as shown by their willingness to pay that amount to acquire it. Additional cartons of soda are not produced, because they do not provide mutual benefit to consumers and producers. Although a 101st carton could be produced at a cost of $10, no consumer is willing to pay that price for another carton. While the additional carton would have some value to consumers, the value is not great enough to make it worthwhile for producers to supply it. The market reaches an efficient outcome, as all production that is mutually beneficial for consumers and producers takes place and no other production takes place. In short, the market achieves all of the potential gains from free exchange.

Introducing a tax on soda changes this benign picture by creating an excess burden. Suppose that a $2-per-carton tax is imposed on soda, causing the price to rise to $12.

At this higher price, consumers purchase fewer cartons of soda. Each of the 100 cartons previously purchased must be worth at least $10 to consumers, because consumers purchased them at the $10 price. Not all of them are worth $12 or more, though. Suppose that, at the $12 price, consumers purchase only 90 cartons of soda. In that case, each of the 91st through the 100th cartons must be worth between $10 and $12 to consumers; consumers purchased them when the price was $10, but not when the price was $12.

To understand the full effects of the tax, it is necessary to look both at the 90 cartons that are still produced with the $2 tax in place and at the 10 cartons that are no longer produced with the tax, but were produced when the tax did not exist. As we explain below, the excess burden arises from the impact on the latter 10 cartons. But we first consider the 90 cartons that are still produced and purchased.

For each of these 90 cartons, the gains from free exchange between consumers and producers are still attained. That is certainly good news, as each of these cartons has a value to consumers of $12 or more, and each costs only $10 to produce. Producers continue to receive a net payment of $10 for each of the 90 cartons, while consumers now pay $12 for each of them, including

$2 that goes to the government. The tax raises $180 of revenue.

Although the $180 tax payment is clearly a burden on consumers, it is not "necessarily" a burden on society as a whole. It is instead a transfer of resources from consumers to the government. The government can use the $180 revenue to provide goods and services to the public, which can offset the burden of the tax payments. It can even offset the burden by simply returning the money. Of course, the government may fail to use the revenue properly, in which case the taxpayers suffer a net burden. Any such burden is caused by bad spending policy, though, rather than by the tax itself.

In this book, we focus on another burden imposed by the soda tax, which is in excess of the tax payments and is therefore referred to as the excess burden. (In public finance textbooks, excess burden is sometimes called deadweight loss or welfare cost.) As explained below, the excess burden is pure waste because it raises no revenue for the government. A net burden is unavoidable because the government receives no money with which it can provide services or benefits. No matter how wise its spending policies may be, the government cannot offset this excess burden, as it could with the tax payments. In that sense, the excess burden is the real tax burden.

The excess burden is related to the 10 cartons of soda that are no longer produced and purchased. Although the production and sale of those 10 cartons was mutually advantageous to consumers and producers, these trades no longer occur when the tax is in place. Each of those 10 cartons has a value to consumers of at least $10; we know this because consumers purchased them when the price was $10. But none has a value exceeding $12; we know that because consumers refrain from purchasing them when the price rises to $12. Because each carton costs $10 to produce, consumers received a net gain of somewhere between zero and $2 from the purchase of each of these cartons.

Those gains from trade are destroyed when the tax prevents these cartons of soda from being produced and purchased. The failure of these mutually beneficial transactions to occur is an example of economic inefficiency, because it makes the consumers worse off without making anyone else better off. The problem is that the tax interferes with the freedom of consumers and producers to engage in mutually beneficial exchange, as engaging in such exchanges would trigger additional tax liability.

In other words, the excess burden arises because the tax changes the incentives confronting consumers. The tax gives consumers an artificial incentive to avoid purchasing soda, because their tax liability goes down when they buy fewer cartons. Unfortunately, responding to this incentive prevents mutually beneficial transactions between consumers and producers from taking place.

It is easy to compute the approximate dollar value of excess burden. As mentioned above, the net loss is somewhere between zero and $2 for each of the 10 cartons driven out of production. So, the average loss per carton is likely to be around $1, implying that the total excess burden is approximately $10. Consumers therefore experience a $190 loss from the tax, consisting of the $180 tax payment, which may be returned to them in some form, and the $10 excess burden, which is unavoidably wasted. The appendix to this chapter shows how the excess burden can be graphed using supply and demand curves.

The excess burden differs from "burdens" that are often discussed in political debate. In this example, the tax reduces producers' receipts by $100, because the 10 cartons that are no longer produced had been sold for $10 each before the tax was introduced. The workers and other producers in the soda industry have therefore lost $100 of income, due to the contraction of their industry from the tax. This $100 loss is not a burden, though, because the income merely compensated the workers and other producers for the sacrifices they incurred to take part in soda production. The only real burden is the forgone benefits that consumers would have received from these 10 cartons of soda.

The difference between revenue and burden is particularly clear-cut when the tax is so high that it completely drives out the activity that is taxed. Suppose that, in the above example, imposing a $30-per-carton tax would cause no soda at all to be produced, because no carton of soda offers consumers a net benefit of $30 or more. If we focus only on revenue, adopting a $30 tax looks the same as having no tax, because the government collects no revenue in either case. In reality, though, the outcome with the $30 tax is far worse than the outcome with no soda tax because the $30 tax creates a large burden. With no tax, consumers enjoy the full benefits of free exchange with producers; with the $30 tax, consumers enjoy none of the benefits of free exchange. Because the tax raises no revenue, the entire burden of the tax takes the form of excess burden.

BEHAVIORAL SENSITIVITY AND EXCESS BURDEN

A key factor determining the size of the excess burden is the sensitivity of behavior to prices. For example, if the $2 tax had caused soda demand to fall by 20 cartons rather than by 10, the excess burden would have been twice as large.

If soda is a luxury that consumers will readily stop buying as prices rise, the excess burden is large; if it is a necessity that consumers will cut back on very little as prices rise, the excess burden is small. At first glance, it may seem odd that the smallest excess burden is associated with the tax that is the hardest to avoid. Isn't a tax that is difficult to avoid more, rather than less, burdensome? As explained below, such a tax is indeed more burdensome in some respects, yet it actually has smaller excess burden.

To understand how this works, introduce a second group of consumers into the example. Like the first group of consumers, they buy 100 cartons of soda when there is no tax and the price is $10. Unlike the first group, though, these consumers view soda as essential to life itself, so they continue to buy the same 100 cartons even if the price rises sharply. The imposition of the $2 tax raises $200 revenue from this group. Because they do not change their behavior to avoid the tax, there is no excess burden. The total burden of the tax on this group is $200, equal to the revenue raised by the tax.

How does this compare to the burden on the first group of consumers? Recall that the tax raised only $180 revenue from them, because they cut back their soda purchases to 90 cartons in response to the tax. We saw that this reduction in purchases caused an excess burden of approximately $10, yielding a total burden of roughly $190.

So, it is true that the first group of consumers, for whom the tax is easier to avoid, bears a smaller total burden, $190 rather than $200. Just as intuition suggests, the ability to avoid the tax results in a smaller burden. Yet, it is precisely this ability to avoid the tax that results in a larger excess burden on the first group. Although a tax that is easier to avoid imposes a smaller total burden, it raises less revenue and the excess burden—the portion of the burden that doesn't result in revenue—is actually larger.

In the extreme case, a tax that is impossible to avoid has no excess burden at all. This occurs when the tax is "lump sum," meaning that the size of each individual's tax does not depend on any decision that he or she makes. A lump-sum tax may be a fixed amount for all individuals, or it may vary across individuals based on personal characteristics that individuals are unable to change. Because the individuals cannot do anything to change the amount of tax, they make no behavioral changes to avoid the tax. The only burden is then the tax payment itself, and there is no excess burden from behavioral changes.

We now need to consider one of the most technical aspects of excess burden. This issue is of little importance to the excess burden of the soda tax, but will be critical in understanding the excess burden of the wage, income, and consumption taxes discussed in subsequent chapters.

As explained above, excess burden arises from behavioral changes that are made to avoid the tax. In computing excess burden, we therefore ignore behavioral changes that arise simply because the tax makes the consumer poorer. The latter tax changes occur even with a lump-sum tax. For example, if the consumer is told that she must pay a lump-sum tax of $100 no matter how much soda she buys, she cannot and will not change her soda purchases *in order to avoid the tax*. But she will presumably reduce her soda purchases, along with her purchases of everything else, because she has $100 less to spend. That response is not part of the excess burden, because it is part of the burden of the tax payment itself.

In technical terms, we do not compute the excess burden of the soda tax by looking at the reduction in soda purchases relative to the outcome with no taxes. Instead, we look at the reduction in soda purchases relative to the outcome with a lump-sum tax that is equally burdensome, which measures the reduction in purchases caused by changes in incentives.

We should note that behavioral sensitivity is not the only factor that determines the size of a tax's excess burden. As one would expect, the tax rate is also important.

TAX RATE AND EXCESS BURDEN

All else being equal, the excess burden is higher when the tax rate is higher. In fact, the rate of increase is stronger than one might expect. When the tax rate is doubled, the excess burden does not merely double, but roughly quadruples. As we will explain below, the excess burden is approximately proportional to the square of the tax rate.

To see why this is the case, let's return to the example used earlier. In the above example, doubling the soda tax from $2 per carton to $4 increases the excess burden from roughly $10 to roughly $40. While the original $2 tax caused a $10 excess burden, the $2 tax increase is three times as harmful, causing an additional $30 of excess burden.

Why does this happen? It's not because the tax increase has a bigger impact than the original tax on the amount of soda purchased. For simplicity, we assume that consumer demand for soda declines at a fixed rate as the price rises, so that each $2 additional tax triggers an additional reduction of 10 cartons. Just as the original $2 tax, which raised the consumer price from $10 to $12, was assumed to reduce purchases by 10 cartons, from 100 to 90, so the $2 tax increase, which raises the price from $12 to $14, is assumed to reduce purchases by another 10 cartons, from 90 to 80.

The $2 tax increase is more harmful than the original $2 tax, even though both drive 10 cartons of soda out of the market. The reason is that not all cartons of soda are worth the same amount to consumers. The cartons driven out by the tax increase are significantly more valuable than those driven out by the original tax; in fact, their greater value is confirmed by the fact that they withstood the introduction of the original tax.

Recall that each of the 10 cartons of soda driven out by the original tax offered a net gain to consumers of somewhere between zero and $2 (based on the fact that the consumers purchased each of these cartons at the $10 price, but not at the $12 price), for an average net gain per carton of about $1. In contrast, each of the 10 cartons driven out by the tax increase was purchased at the $12 price, but is no longer purchased at the $14 price. So, each of these cartons must be worth between $12 and $14 to consumers, and the net gain from producing each carton at a cost of $10 must lie somewhere between $2 and $4. The average net gain per carton is about $3, and the excess burden from driving these 10 cartons out of the market is therefore about $30.

The $2 tax increase not only imposes larger excess burden than the original $2 tax but also raises less revenue for the government. With the original $2 tax, 90 cartons of soda were purchased, and revenue was $180. With the tax raised to $4, 80 cartons are purchased, and revenue is $320. So, the original $2 tax raised $180 of revenue and inflicted $10 of excess burden, but the $2 tax increase raises only $140 of additional revenue while inflicting $30 of additional excess burden.

The pattern continues as the tax rate rises, with each tax increase causing more excess burden and raising less additional revenue than the preceding one. For example, another $2 tax increase (raising the tax to $6 and the price to $16 and reducing soda production to 70 cartons) would raise only $100 of additional revenue while inflicting $50 of additional excess burden.

This pattern has important tax policy implications. The analysis suggests that it is possible to raise moderate amounts of revenue with only modest excess burden. That is fortunate, because it is necessary to raise some revenue to finance essential public services. We should be cautious about pushing taxes too high, though, as doing so may impose large increases in excess burden relative to the additional revenue that is raised.

EXCESS BURDEN OF SUBSIDIES

Subsidies, as well as taxes, have an excess burden. Although the analysis for subsidies may initially seem counterintuitive in some respects, we will see that the underlying logic is the same as for taxes, with excess burden again arising from interference with mutually beneficial exchange.

Consider a $2 per carton subsidy to soda, which drives the price down to $8 per carton. Under our assumption that changes in the price change demand at a fixed rate, this price decline causes 110 cartons to be purchased and sold. The subsidy then has a budgetary cost of $220. Although consumers receive a benefit from the subsidy, their benefit is smaller than the $220 that the government spends on the subsidy. This shortfall is referred to as the excess burden of the subsidy, although it arguably should be called the "deficient benefit."

The excess burden does not arise from the first 100 cartons of soda, which were produced without the subsidy and continue to be produced with it. For each of those cartons, the government spends $2 on the subsidy and the consumer gains $2 by paying an $8 price rather than a $10 price. For these cartons, the government spends $200, and the consumer gains the full $200, with no excess burden.

Instead, the excess burden arises from the 10 newly produced cartons. Just as with the excess burden of the tax, the excess burden of the subsidy arises from the change in behavior resulting from the new incentives.

For each of these 10 cartons, the government spends $2 on the subsidy, but the consumer gains less than $2. Because consumers did not buy any of these cartons when the price was $10, but do buy them when the price is $8, each carton must be worth somewhere between $8 and $10 to the consumer. When the subsidy allows a consumer to buy each of the cartons at a price of $8, the net gain to the consumer must be somewhere between zero and $2. The average net gain is about $1 per carton, so the consumer gains roughly $10 from the subsidy to these 10 newly produced cartons. On these cartons, the government spends $20, but the consumer gains only $10, leaving a $10 excess burden.

It is no coincidence that the $2 subsidy has the same $10 excess burden as the $2 tax. The tax and the subsidy are mirror images of each other. All of the key points about the excess burden of taxes carry over to the excess burden of subsidies. As with taxes, doubling the subsidy quadruples the excess burden. Also, as with the tax, the excess burden of the subsidy is larger if demand is more sensitive to the price.

The excess burden of the tax is so similar to the excess burden of the subsidy because both burdens have the same fundamental economic explanation. The tax imposes an excess burden because it prevents transactions that are mutually beneficial (in the absence of the tax) from being undertaken. The subsidy imposes an excess burden because it induces transactions that are not mutually beneficial (in the absence of the subsidy) to be undertaken. Yet, even this parallelism fails to fully capture the similarity. When a tax prevents beneficial transactions, nonbeneficial transactions arise to replace them in the economy. When a subsidy induces nonbeneficial transactions, they replace beneficial transactions in the economy. In the end, the tax and the subsidy have exactly the same flaw—each of them channels economic transactions away from beneficial to nonbeneficial forms, as consumers respond to the incentive to pay fewer taxes or to collect more subsidies.

With a subsidy, even more than with a tax, it is important to realize that excess burden reflects a loss of the gains from mutually beneficial exchange rather than a simple output reduction. After all, the $2 subsidy actually increases soda production from 100 to 110 cartons, bringing in $100 of additional income for producers. That additional income is not a net gain to society, however, because it merely compensates the producers for the labor and other costs of producing the 10 additional cartons. Because the cartons cost $100 to produce while providing only $90 of benefits to consumers, this increase in output is actually a net burden rather than a gain. The purpose of economic activity is not to mindlessly increase output of particular products but to meet consumer needs through mutually beneficial exchange. Subsidies, no less than taxes, impede that purpose by introducing artificial incentives that change behavior and drive consumers and producers away from mutually beneficial transactions.

OTHER ISSUES IN EXCESS BURDEN

Public finance textbooks discuss several other issues related to excess burden. Due to space limitations, we mention them only briefly here.

One important issue concerns externalities, which are side effects on third parties caused by the production or consumption of a good. For example, suppose that the production of each carton of soda causes pollution, thereby harming people other than the consumers and producers. Then, soda production that benefits both the producer and the consumer may not actually represent a beneficial exchange, due to the harm to third parties. In that case, imposing a tax on soda production (or on the pollution that it causes) can be desirable (in other words, have a negative excess burden). The same logic can justify a subsidy to an activity that has beneficial effects on third parties. Taxes and subsidies that correct problems of this kind are called corrective taxes and subsidies. (They are also sometimes called Pigovian taxes and subsidies, in honor of Arthur Cecil Pigou, the economist who first discussed them.) In chapter 4, when we discuss how income tax provisions that reward or penalize certain types of behavior can cause excess burden, we will consider the possibility that a few of the provisions may be justified as corrective taxes or subsidies.

Complicated issues arise when more than one tax is in place. If another product that is a close substitute for soda, perhaps juice, is already taxed, that tax causes excess burden by reducing purchases of juice. If juice and soda are substitutes, then the reduction in juice purchases triggers increased purchases of soda. If there is no way to remove the juice tax, then placing a tax on soda may have negative excess burden. The reason is that the soda tax reduces soda purchases and triggers an increase in purchases of the juice substitute, thereby undoing some of the effects of the juice tax and canceling out some of the excess burden it causes. The interaction of different taxes in increasing or reducing excess burden can be very complicated. In general, taxes on specific goods like soda or juice have larger excess burdens than taxes on broader categories such as beverages.

Other complications arise if the cost of producing each carton of soda rises as more cartons are produced, rather than remaining constant at $10, as we have assumed.

SUMMARY

Tax payments are the most obvious burden arising from a tax. But economists actually devote more attention to the excess burden, which is the cost imposed on taxpayers as they change their behavior to avoid the tax. In a sense, the excess burden is the real tax burden. Unlike the tax payments, which are transferred to the government and can potentially be returned to taxpayers in some form, the excess burden is pure waste, reflecting the loss of the gains from mutually beneficial exchanges between consumers and producers. A subsidy causes excess burden in the same way as a tax.

We have discussed a soda tax only to introduce the key concepts. We are now ready to discuss the excess burden of wage, consumption, and income taxes, which are the taxes from which governments actually obtain most of their revenue.

APPENDIX: GRAPHING EXCESS BURDEN WITH SUPPLY-AND-DEMAND CURVES

As discussed in public finance textbooks, excess burden can be graphed using supply and demand curves. Familiarity with such curves, including the distinction between compensated and ordinary demand curves, is assumed in this appendix.

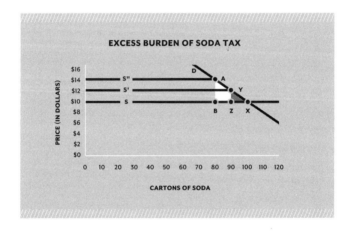

The original $2 tax on soda shifts the supply curve from S to S'. The demand curve D is unaffected. The excess burden of this tax is the triangle XYZ, which has an area of $10.

Increasing the tax to $4 shifts the supply curve to S''. The total excess burden of the $4 tax is the triangle XAB, which has an area of $40. The additional excess burden from the tax increase is the area ABYZ, which is $30.

To isolate the changes in purchases due to the incentive effects, we assume that the demand curve shown in the figure is the compensated demand curve.

2

**EXCESS BURDEN OF
WAGE, INCOME, AND
CONSUMPTION TAXES**

We now use the principles outlined in the previous chapter to examine the excess burden of wage, income, and consumption taxes, the primary types of broad-based taxes used in the United States and other countries. A wage tax has a similar structure to an income tax, but the wage tax applies only to labor income, such as salaries and bonuses, not to capital income, such as interest, dividends, or capital gains. The primary example of a wage tax in the federal tax system is the payroll tax, which we will discuss in chapter 3. The United States does not have a broad consumption tax at the federal level, although many state and local governments impose consumption taxes in the form of retail sales taxes.

As explained below, one of the major sources of excess burden for the income tax, and the primary way in which it differs from wage and consumption taxes is the penalty it places on saving. Because the impact on saving is so important, we set it aside for separate discussion at the end of the chapter and begin by looking at the excess burden of wage, income, and consumption taxes in a world with no need or opportunity to save for future years.

WAGE, INCOME, AND CONSUMPTION TAXES IN A NO-SAVING WORLD

Even in this no-saving world, individuals have a number of economic decisions to make, and taxes affect those decisions in ways that give rise to excess burden. One key decision is how much time to devote to leisure and how much time to devote to work. Because working provides wages that are used to buy consumer goods, either immediately or later, this choice is really between leisure and consumption. We focus on how taxes affect this decision, before turning to the impact of taxes on other decisions.

All of the taxes discussed in this chapter—wage, income, and consumption taxes—are taxes on work. An individual who spends all of his time enjoying leisure does not generate any income to consume and therefore does not pay any of these three taxes. In contrast, an individual who works will earn wages, which are a form of income, and will consume them, either immediately or later, thereby incurring a tax liability under any of these three tax systems.

We saw that a tax on soda has an excess burden because individuals buy less soda to avoid the tax. In just the same way, a tax on work has an excess burden because individuals work less to avoid the tax. Excess burden is computed in the same manner as for the soda tax.

For example, consider a taxpayer with a $10-per-hour wage, who would work 100 hours, to earn and consume $1,000, in the absence of a tax on work. Suppose that she chooses to work only 80 hours and earn only $800 under a 40 percent flat-wage tax or income tax. She does this because the final 20 hours of work are no longer worth it when she can keep only $6 per hour, although they were worth it when she was allowed to keep her full $10-per-hour wage.

In this case, the 40 percent income tax raises $320 of revenue from the $800 of wages that the worker still earns. In addition to the $320 tax payment, the taxpayer suffers an excess burden by forgoing the opportunity to earn the final $200. Because each of those dollars was earned when the entire dollar could be retained but not when only 60 cents could be retained, earning each dollar must have imposed a cost (in terms of giving up leisure) of somewhere between 60 cents and a dollar, with the average cost likely to be about 80 cents. The taxpayer would have gained an average of about 20 cents on the dollar by earning each of these 200 dollars, so the tax imposes approximately $40 of excess burden.

The other principles discussed in the soda tax example also apply to the income tax. For example, the excess burden approximately quadruples if the tax rate is doubled. Also, the excess burden is larger if taxpayers change their behavior more to avoid the tax.

The latter fact may call into question whether taxes on work have a large excess burden. After all, many individuals may not change their work decision much in response to changes in wage, income, and consumption tax rates. Indeed, might not some individuals work more when tax rates go up, because they need additional income in order to be able to pay the tax while still enjoying a decent standard of living?

At this point, it is necessary to recall the technical concept introduced in chapter 1—excess burden depends on the behavioral change *that is made to avoid the tax*. The relevant comparison is how work changes under a wage, income, or consumption tax, compared to an equally burdensome lump-sum tax, which cannot be avoided by working less. An individual who works roughly the same under a 40 percent wage tax as he would with no tax at all is likely to be working far less than he would if he had to pay a lump-sum tax equal to 40 percent of his income.

Many labor economists have performed statistical studies to estimate how sensitive work decisions are to tax rates. Economist Nada Eissa recently observed that these studies generally find that different groups in the population respond differently to tax rates. In particular, tax rates have little effect on the number of hours that men work, but have significant effects on married women's decisions about whether to work.

Perhaps more important, wage, income, and consumption taxes are not just taxes on work. They would be nothing more than taxes on work if they applied at the same rate to all of the compensation that a person received for working, no matter in what form it was received or how it was used. In that case, the only behavioral change that could be made to avoid the tax, and therefore the only source of excess burden, would be a reduction in work. But actual wage, income, and consumption taxes are not designed that way.

As we will explain in chapter 3, income tax liability in the current U.S. tax system depends on the manner in which people are paid for their work and the way in which they spend their money. Some types of behavior are rewarded by the tax code with exclusions, deductions, and credits, while others are not. As a result, taxpayers can reduce their tax payments not only by working less but also by arranging to be paid in tax-preferred form, spending their money on tax-preferred activities, or engaging in tax evasion. As we will explain in chapter 4, those behavioral changes also give rise to excess burden.

So far, we have seen that wage, income, and consumption taxes all impose excess burden by prompting individuals to work less or to channel their income into forms or uses that are tax exempt. As we mentioned at the beginning of this chapter, income taxes, though not wage taxes and consumption taxes, also impose excess burden by penalizing saving.

THE INCOME TAX PENALIZES SAVING

To understand the income tax's penalty on saving, consider two individuals, Patient and Impatient, each of whom earns $100 of wages today. Impatient wishes to consume only today, whereas Patient wishes to consume only at a future date. Savings can be invested by firms in machines that yield a 100 percent rate of return between now and the (potentially distant) future date. In a world with no taxes, Impatient consumes $100 today. Patient lends the $100 to a firm, which buys a machine that yields a $200 payoff in the future. At that time, the firm pays Patient back her $100 loan and $100 interest, allowing her to consume $200.

What happens in a world with a 20 percent income

tax? Impatient pays a $20 tax on his wages and consumes the remaining $80, which is 20 percent less than in the no-tax world. Patient also pays a $20 tax and lends the remaining $80 to a firm. On her $80 loan, she eventually earns $80 interest, for a total of $160. However, because a $16 tax is imposed on the $80 interest income, Patient is left with only $144 to consume.

Patient's $144 consumption is 28 percent less than the $200 she consumes in the no-tax world. In comparison, the income tax reduced Impatient's consumption by a mere 20 percent. Under the income tax, Patient faces a higher percentage tax burden than Impatient solely because she saves for future consumption rather than consuming today.

Some economists refer to the savings penalty under the income tax as a "double tax" because tax is collected twice—first on wages and then on the return to savings. Whether or not we use this terminology, though, what matters is that the income tax places a higher effective tax rate on future consumption than on current consumption.

By discouraging saving, the income tax introduces another source of excess burden. This excess burden is fundamentally the same as the other excess burdens we have discussed—people change their behavior to avoid the tax, in this case by saving less. Once again, excess burden is a loss of the gains from free exchange, in this case the exchange between savers and firms.

We explained above that wage, income, and

consumption taxes necessarily cause excess burden by penalizing work relative to leisure. We further noted that the actual U.S. income tax system creates further excess burden, to be detailed in chapters 3 and 4, by also linking tax liability to the form in which the income from work is received and the manner in which it is used. A parallel point applies here.

An income tax necessarily imposes an additional source of excess burden by penalizing saving relative to current consumption. However, the U.S. individual and corporate income tax system creates further excess burden by also linking tax liability to the manner in which the saving and investment are financed and the assets and industries in which the investment occurs. We detail these points in chapters 3 and 5.

WAGE AND CONSUMPTION TAXES DO NOT PENALIZE SAVING

Wage taxes and consumption taxes do not penalize saving and therefore avoid that source of excess burden, even though they do penalize work, as previously discussed.

The wage tax does not penalize saving and does not collect any revenue from saving. In the above example, with a 20 percent wage tax, Patient and Impatient both pay a $20 tax today. Patient invests her remaining $80, allowing her to consume $160 at the future date, while Impatient consumes his remaining $80 today, so both experience the same 20 percent reduction in consumption. The wage tax therefore does not penalize saving. Unlike with the income tax, taxpayers cannot reduce their tax burden by saving less, eliminating that source of excess burden.

Consumption taxation also yields a neutral outcome if the tax rate remains constant over time. Consider a 20 percent consumption tax (actually one where the tax is 20 percent of the combined amount that is consumed and paid in tax). After earning $100 of wages, Impatient consumes $80 and pays a $20 tax, where the $20 tax is 20 percent of $100 (the $80 consumption plus the $20 tax).

Patient lends her entire $100 to the firm; she owes no tax because she has not yet consumed. On her $100 loan, she earns $100 interest, accumulating $200. In the future, she consumes $160 and pays a $40 tax, where the $40 tax is 20 percent of $200 (the $160 consumption plus the $40 tax). Each worker's consumption is reduced by 20 percent relative to a world with no taxes. Because both workers face the same percentage tax burden, the consumption tax does not penalize saving. As with the wage tax, and unlike with the income tax, taxpayers cannot reduce their tax burden by saving less, eliminating that type of excess burden.

Although a consumption tax does not impose a penalty on saving, it can collect two types of revenue from saving, which we have not yet discussed. First, a consumption tax collects revenue from above-normal returns. Suppose, in the above example, that the machine is unusually productive and yields $220 rather than the $200 minimum required to make the investment worthwhile. The extra return is taxed. Second, if no transition relief is offered, the consumption tax collects revenue from saving that was done before the tax was introduced. If a machine is already in place when the consumption tax was introduced (there was none in the example), its output is taxed when consumed.

These two types of revenue collection generally do not result in a penalty on saving. The former taxes away only part of the surplus return, over and above the minimum needed to motivate the saving. The latter applies only to saving that has already taken place, so it has no incentive effects, unless the adoption of the consumption tax was anticipated when the saving was done or unless it prompts savers to anticipate future policy changes that will reduce their after-tax rates of return.

Because consumption taxes collect this additional revenue that wage taxes do not collect, most economists view consumption taxes as superior to wage taxes. Proposals to eliminate the saving penalty, and the associated excess burden, imposed by income taxes therefore generally look to consumption rather than wage, taxes as the solution. In chapter 6, we will discuss several possible ways to tax consumption.

SAVING AND ECONOMIC GROWTH

The income tax penalty on saving not only causes excess burden but also impedes long-run economic growth. An economy can increase its output over time only by using better technology to turn inputs into output or by increasing its inputs. One of the primary inputs used in production is capital, such as plant and equipment, which is financed by saving. Without saving to finance the building of plant and equipment, long-run economic growth is greatly diminished.

A common misconception holds that consumption, rather than saving, is good for the economy because consumer spending creates jobs. This misconception confuses short-term economic fluctuations in performance (or underperformance) of the economy with long-run growth. Increasing consumption at appropriate times can help smooth out short-term fluctuations, but persistent increases in consumption are harmful.

Economies are often subject to fluctuations in which booms are followed by recessions, in which many workers lose their jobs. The government can smooth out these cycles by increasing the economy's aggregate demand for goods during bad times and reducing demand during good times. When the economy is in recession, a quick way to boost the economy is to temporarily increase consumer spending. And when the economy is overheated, a quick way to restrain it is to temporarily reduce consumer spending. Regardless of how the timing of consumer spending is manipulated to smooth the business cycle, though, long-run growth is strongest when more resources are devoted to investment for the future rather than to current consumer spending. Policies that discourage savings—and thereby encourage consumption—inhibit long-run economic growth.

SUMMARY

Wage, income, and consumption taxes create excess burden by discouraging work. Income taxes create further excess burden by discouraging saving. As detailed below, the actual U.S. income tax system causes still more excess burden by discouraging particular ways of receiving and spending income and particular ways of financing and making investments. To illustrate these points, we now turn to a discussion of the actual U.S. tax system.

3

TAXATION IN THE UNITED STATES: AN OVERVIEW

In the first two chapters, we introduced the concept of excess burden and explained the excess burden of wage, consumption, and income taxes. Having established this foundation, we now turn to the actual U.S. tax system. We begin by examining the history of the U.S. tax system and its various components—individual and corporate income taxes, payroll taxes, excise taxes, and estate and gift taxes—in order to understand how they came to exist in their current forms.

Today, virtually all working Americans have direct experience with the federal tax system in the form of income and payroll taxes, but this was not always the case. In fact, the U.S. tax system as we know it today did not exist until the twentieth century. For well over a century after the American founding, duties, tariffs, and various excise taxes (taxes on the sale of specific goods) were the federal government's primary sources of revenue.

TAX POLICY IS NO LONGER SIMPLY ABOUT REVENUE COLLECTION, BUT HAS BECOME A MEANS TO REDISTRIBUTE INCOME AND INFLUENCE BEHAVIOR.

The issue of taxes was a primary reason for the American Revolution against British rule, as the American colonists famously rallied against "taxation without representation." Taxes have remained a sensitive subject in American politics to this day. Since the nation's founding, however, the expansion of the federal government, U.S. involvement in foreign and domestic wars, government responses to economic downturns, and the creation of social insurance programs have enlarged and shaped the tax system to varying degrees. As we will see, tax policy is no longer simply about revenue collection, but has become a means to redistribute income and influence behavior.

The most significant expansions of the U.S. tax system were the institution of corporate income taxes in 1909, individual income taxes in 1913, and payroll taxes in 1935. Over time, the distribution of revenue sources has shifted, as table 1 demonstrates. Since the early 1940s, the individual income tax has been the cornerstone of the U.S. tax system. After 1950, the corporate income tax declined steadily as a share of revenue, while the

TABLE 1. HISTORICAL TRENDS IN FEDERAL REVENUE SOURCES

	1950	1975	2000	2010
Individual Income Tax	40%	44%	50%	42%
Corporate Income Tax	26%	15%	10%	9%
Payroll Tax	11%	30%	32%	40%
Excise Taxes	19%	6%	3%	3%
Other	3%	5%	5%	7%

Source: U.S. Office of Management and Budget, Historical Tables, Table 2.1, "Receipts by Source: 1934–2015."

share of payroll taxes greatly increased. The payroll tax first surpassed the corporate income tax as a source of revenue in 1968 and is now a close second to the individual income tax. By 1975, the share of revenue raised by excise taxes—once a major source of federal revenue—had drastically decreased. To offer a better understanding of the shifts in and development of the tax system, we turn now to these various components of the federal tax system. For simplicity, we do not discuss state and local taxes.

INDIVIDUAL INCOME TAX

Although income tax was collected briefly during the Civil War, the individual income tax was not introduced on a permanent basis until 1913. However, the income tax did not affect many Americans until it was expanded in the 1940s in response to the fiscal demands of World War II. The number of Americans subject to income taxation jumped from four million in 1939 to forty-three million in 1945.

The individual income tax is a progressive tax, which means that the ratio of taxes paid to amount of income increases with income. In 2010, it accounted for 42 percent of federal revenue. Every facet of the individual income tax has evolved over its roughly one century of existence, including who is taxed, how much of their income is taxed, at what rate, and how the tax is paid. In this section, we provide a brief overview of this important tax's current form. In chapter 4, we will

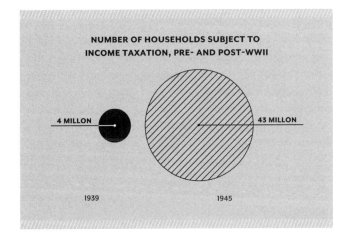

NUMBER OF HOUSEHOLDS SUBJECT TO INCOME TAXATION, PRE- AND POST-WWII

4 MILLON

43 MILLON

1939

1945

discuss in depth issues related to personal taxation, including excess burden.

Filing Status. Before calculating the amount of tax owed, the taxpayer must determine his or her filing status. There are five categories for filing status: single, married filing jointly, married filing separately, head of household, and widow(er) with dependent child. Heads of household are unmarried individuals who pay more than half the cost of taking care of themselves and a dependent.

Computation of Tax. An important step in computing tax liability is adjusted gross income (AGI), which includes wages, interest, dividends, capital gains, alimony received, rental income, royalties, unemployment compensation, and income from retirement accounts. Contributions to health savings accounts and individual retirement accounts, alimony paid, and certain business expenses, among other types of expenditures, are subtracted in the computation of AGI. The amount of tax an individual pays, however, is based not on AGI but on taxable income, which is AGI minus personal exemptions and deductions.

Personal exemptions and deductions allow taxpayers to subtract specific amounts from their income before calculating how much tax they owe. A taxpayer can generally claim a personal exemption for one's self, as well as one for a spouse and one each for any children or dependents. The personal exemption amount for 2011 is $3,700.

In addition, taxpayers may deduct various items from AGI, including charitable contributions, interest paid on home mortgages, and state and local income and property taxes, among others. Since 1944, taxpayers have had the option, in lieu of itemizing these deductions, to simply subtract from AGI a predetermined amount known as the standard deduction. For 2011, the standard deduction is $5,800 for individuals, $11,600 for married couples filing jointly, and $8,500 for heads of households. A taxpayer who is elderly or blind may add an additional $1,150 if married, or $1,450 if single, to his or her standard deduction.

TABLE 2. 2011 INDIVIDUAL INCOME TAX RATES

MARGINAL TAX RATE	MARRIED FILING JOINTLY	MARRIED FILING SEPARATELY	SINGLE	HEAD OF HOUSEHOLD
10%	$0-$17,000	$0-$8,500	$0-$8,500	$0-$12,150
15%	$17,001-$69,000	$8,501-$34,500	$8,501-$34,500	$12,151-$46,250
25%	$69,001-#139,350	$34,501-$69,675	$34,501-$83,600	$46,251-$119,400
28%	$139,351-$212,300	$69,676-$106,150	$83,601-$174,400	$119,401-$193,350
33%	$212,301-$379,150	$106,151-$189,575	$174,401-$379,150	$193,351-$379,150
35%	$379,151+	$189,576+	$379,151+	$379,151+

Source: Internal Revenue Procudure 2011–12.

After deductions and exemptions have been subtracted to obtain taxable income, taxpayers calculate the amount of tax they owe by consulting the rate schedule for the category in which they are filing. In each rate schedule, tax brackets divide income into segments, and each segment is taxed at a different marginal rate, which is the rate applied to the last dollar of income earned. As table 2 shows, in each rate schedule, income is divided into six brackets, with marginal tax rates ranging from 10 percent to 35 percent. The marginal tax rate for the top tax bracket peaked at 94 percent in 1994.

Two types of income—dividends received by shareholders on stocks and long-term capital gains (profits from the sale of assets, such as stocks or property, held for longer than one year)—are taxed at their own tax rate structure. In general, dividends and capital gains currently are taxed at 15 percent for taxpayers whose ordinary marginal tax rate is 25 percent or higher and taxed at a zero rate for taxpayers in the 10 or 15 percent brackets.

A common misconception is that, when a taxpayer moves into a higher bracket, her entire taxable income is taxed at that higher rate. In reality, as noted above, the new tax rate applies only to the portion of the income that falls into that bracket. For example, although a single taxpayer with $80,000 of taxable income is in the 25 percent bracket, her tax liability is not $20,000. Instead, it is $16,125, which arises because the first $8,500 of taxable income is taxed at 10 percent, the next $26,000 is taxed at 15 percent, and (only) the final $45,500 is taxed at 25 percent. Yet, the taxpayer faces a 25 percent *marginal* tax rate, because she will pay 25 cents additional tax if she earns an additional dollar of taxable income.

EXAMPLE: THE SMITHS'S TAX RETURN

Meet John and Mary Smith. They have one child, Tommy. John and Mary file federal income taxes jointly. Each spouse made $55,000 in 2011. Each contributed $5,000 to an IRA retirement account, making their combined adjusted gross income $100,000. When filing their federal tax return, they claim the $3,700 personal exemption for themselves and for Tommy, totaling $11,100.

They give to charity and pay state and local income taxes and could deduct these from their AGI, but they do not own a home and therefore do not have mortgage payments for which they could deduct interest paid, an amount that, together with the other deductions, would likely exceed the standard deduction. Because the deductions they could itemize do not exceed the standard deduction of $11,600 allowable for married couples filing jointly, they take the standard deduction.

After claiming the personal exemptions and the standard deduction, their taxable income is $77,300 ($100,000 AGI – $11,100 personal exemptions – $11,600 standard deduction).

To compute the tax they owe, they consult the rate schedule for married couples filing jointly. Their first $17,000 of income is taxed at 10 percent; their income between the top of the first bracket and $69,000 is taxed at 15 percent; and their income between the top of the second bracket and $77,300 is taxed at 25 percent. The amount of tax they owe is: ($17,000 x 0.1) + ($52,000 x 0.15) + ($8,300 x 0.25) = $11,575.

However, their return is not yet complete, because they can claim the $1,000 child tax credit for Tommy. So their actual federal income tax liability is $10,575. Depending on how much they had withheld from their paychecks during the year, they may still owe part of this amount, or they may get a refund when they file their tax return.

Tax Credits. Taxpayers may claim credit against the tax liability computed above. Tax credits differ from deductions in that they do not reduce taxable income. Instead, a credit is simply subtracted at the end of the calculation from the amount an individual would otherwise owe. Credits are provided for children, college and other higher education costs, child care costs, foreign income taxes, and other items.

Alternative Minimum Tax. Another important feature of the individual income tax is the Alternative Minimum

Tax (AMT), which is separate from the regular individual income tax. The AMT has the same basic structure as the regular individual income tax, but it has different rules at each stage. Taxpayers must pay either their regular income tax or their AMT liability—whichever is larger. The AMT has no standard deduction and disallows some itemized deductions, which usually makes taxable income larger under AMT rules than under the regular income tax system.

Although it was originally intended to tax only the very wealthy, the AMT has spread to more taxpayers because its tax brackets, unlike those of the regular income tax, are not indexed for inflation. To slow this spread, Congress periodically intervenes to provide higher AMT tax-free amounts and temporarily allow certain personal tax credits to be claimed against the AMT. Even so, approximately four million taxpayers were on the AMT in 2009, up from a mere twenty thousand in 1970.

How Tax Is Paid. In the brief period during the Civil War when income tax was collected, taxes on wages were withheld by employers, as they are now. However, for thirty years after the income tax was instituted permanently in 1913, this was not the case. Withholding was not reintroduced until the ratification of the Current Tax Payment Act of 1943. Although the withholding of income taxes at the source has sometimes been criticized for making the income tax burden less visible to taxpayers, it has clearly led to streamlined administration and greater compliance.

Individual Income Tax Reform. Two of the most significant legislative changes to individual income taxes in the postwar era occurred under President Ronald Reagan in the 1980s: the Economic Recovery Tax Act of 1981 (ERTA) and the Tax Reform Act of 1986 (TRA86). The driving purpose behind ERTA was to promote economic growth, which was to be achieved through a phased-in 23 percent cut in marginal tax rates. ERTA also indexed standard deductions, personal exemptions, and tax brackets for inflation. TRA86 kept up the reform momentum by further lowering marginal individual income tax rates as well as eliminating and restricting various tax deductions and credits, thereby broadening the tax base. The beginning of the twenty-first century brought another chapter in tax reform with the 2001 and 2003 tax cuts under President George W. Bush, which reduced tax rates on work and investment and expanded tax credits and tax-preferred retirement savings programs. Most of these tax cuts are scheduled to expire on December 31, 2012.

PAYROLL TAXES

Payroll taxes are earmarked to finance Social Security and Medicare Part A, which are intended to provide a safety net for American workers. Federal payroll taxes are legally shared equally between employers and employees, with self-employed individuals responsible for the equivalent of both shares. Implemented with the Social Security Act of 1935 in response to the Great Depression, payroll taxes were initially instated to pay for the newly created Social Security system (and a smaller unemployment insurance program). They were expanded to cover the Medicare Part A program when it was established in 1965. Payroll taxes accounted for 40 percent of revenue in 2010.

Since 1990, employers and employees have each had federal payroll tax rates of 7.65 percent—6.2 percent applied to the first $106,800 (in 2011) of wages for Social Security, and 1.45 percent of all wage earnings (a maximum taxable limit was removed in 1993) for Medicare. However, economists believe that workers generally bear the economic burden of the entire 15.3 percent tax, including the half legally paid by employers.

The payroll tax is often criticized for being regressive, meaning that those with lower incomes pay greater shares of their incomes. However, paying the tax earns a worker direct future benefits from Social Security and Medicare, and the value of these benefits is generally higher relative to tax payments for those with lower wages.

CORPORATE INCOME TAX

The corporate income tax was instituted in 1909, four years before the individual income tax. Corporate income subject to taxation is a company's receipts minus wages, interest on loans, cost of goods sold, and depreciation of capital investments. Companies pay estimated tax on a quarterly basis.

Like the individual income tax, the corporate income tax is also a graduated system with multiple brackets. The top corporate statutory tax rate in the United States has remained at 35 percent since 1993, when it was increased from 34 percent. Because most corporations face this top rate, the corporate tax is often thought of as a flat 35 percent tax. This rate is low compared to corporate tax rates imposed on U.S. corporations in the past—the rate was 52 percent for more than a decade in the 1950s and 1960s and rose to 52.8 percent in 1968–69. But a 35 percent rate is high compared to contemporary rates in other countries, as discussed below.

The U.S. corporate tax system imposes "worldwide" taxation, meaning that all foreign-source income of U.S. companies (those that obtained their corporate charters in the United States) is subject to taxation in the United States. But U.S. companies are allowed a tax credit for foreign income taxes paid on this income. Foreign companies (those that were charted abroad) are subject to U.S. tax on their operations in the United States, but not on their foreign operations.

The corporate income tax's significance in terms of revenue decreased drastically between the 1950s and 1980s. In 2010, only 9 percent of federal revenue came from the corporate income tax. Even so, it remains the third highest source of revenue, after the individual income tax and payroll tax.

Most economists recognize that some type of corporate tax is useful to thwart those who might otherwise hide income in their businesses to avoid the individual income tax. However, this tax has generated substantial controversy, ranging from arguments that its structure causes large excess burden to concerns that workers bear the burden of the tax through lower wages. We will discuss these issues at greater length in chapter 5.

EXCISE, ESTATE, AND GIFT TAXES

Excise taxes, which target specific kinds of consumer goods, comprised only 3 percent of all federal revenue in 2010, while estate and gift taxes, customs duties, and miscellaneous receipts made up 7 percent. This configuration highlights how much the sources of federal revenue have changed; as we noted earlier, the federal government was funded mainly by customs duties and excise taxes at the time of the nation's founding. Indeed, excise taxes were the largest source of federal revenue until 1942. The number of federal excise taxes was cut back significantly in 1965. Today, the main federal excise taxes cover gasoline, air travel, cigarettes, and alcohol. Consumers usually pay these taxes as part of the price of the items they purchase.

Estate and gift taxes target the transfer of wealth and make up a very small portion of federal revenue. The estate tax was instituted in 1916 and is applied in 2011 to estates over $5 million, with a rate schedule ranging from 18 percent up to 35 percent. Gifts over $13,000 per year per recipient are taxed at rates up to 35 percent after a substantial lifetime exemption.

U.S. TAX SYSTEM VERSUS OTHER COUNTRIES

Compared to taxes in other developed countries, U.S. taxes are relatively low. All U.S. taxes (including state and local) were 27.3 percent of gross domestic product (GDP) in 2006, while the average for other countries in the Organisation for Economic Co-operation and Development (OECD) that year was 36.2 percent of GDP. In 2006 the United States ranked fifth-lowest among OECD countries in tax-to-GDP ratios. But tax revenues are only part of the story. The United States is most distinct from other developed countries in how it gets tax revenue. For example, the United States has the second highest corporate tax rate among industrialized countries, largely because other countries have

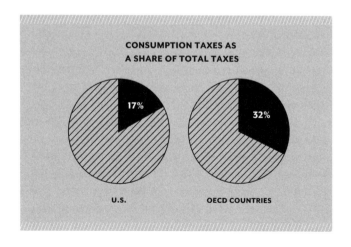

CONSUMPTION TAXES AS
A SHARE OF TOTAL TAXES

17%

32%

U.S.   OECD COUNTRIES

dramatically reduced their rates in recent years, while the U.S. rate has remained constant. In addition, the individual income tax accounts for much more revenue in the United States than in other countries.

Consumption taxes make up a much higher percentage of other countries' revenue than they do in the United States. These taxes brought in an average of 32 percent of total taxes among OECD countries in 2006, whereas the U.S. total (again, including state and local) was only 17 percent. In chapter 6, we will discuss possible reforms that would replace part or all of the income tax system with consumption taxes.

SUMMARY

The current tax system was significantly expanded in the twentieth century, particularly in the postwar era. Since the 1940s, the individual income tax has been the foundation of the U.S. tax system, but payroll taxes as a share of total federal revenue have grown significantly in the last decade. Corporate taxes have declined in significance since the 1950s but have grown in controversy. Excise taxes, once a primary source of federal revenue, now account for a very small share.

The current income tax system, with its progressive rate structure and scores of targeted incentives, reflects the view that, beyond raising revenue, tax policy should be concerned with income redistribution and should encourage or discourage certain behaviors or activities.

4

**ISSUES IN U.S.
PERSONAL INCOME
TAXATION**

> **THE INDIVIDUAL INCOME TAX CAUSES EXCESS BURDEN BECAUSE, BY TAXING WORK, IT AFFECTS AN INDIVIDUAL'S DECISION ABOUT HOW MUCH TO WORK. BUT ALL OF THE OTHER BEHAVIORAL CHANGES THAT PEOPLE CAN MAKE TO CHANGE THEIR INCOME TAX LIABILITY ALSO GIVE RISE TO EXCESS BURDEN.**

In the United States today, the tax code is used not only to generate revenue but also to pursue a host of other policy objectives. An extensive set of credits and deductions, along with income-based limits (phase-ins and phase-outs) on these provisions, subsidize and penalize particular behaviors. Aside from potential inequities, these subsidies and penalties give rise to excess burden as taxpayers change their behavior to lower their tax liability. As we noted in chapter 2, the individual income tax causes excess burden because, by taxing work, it affects an individual's decision about how much to work. But all of the other behavioral changes that people can make to change their income tax liability also give rise to excess burden.

For example, the income tax (and the payroll tax) applies to cash wages, but not to most types of fringe benefits. While working less is one way to avoid this tax and therefore one source of excess burden, receiving fringe benefits rather than cash wages is another way to avoid the tax and therefore another source of excess burden.

The most prominent example is employer-provided health insurance, which is excluded from income tax. This exclusion leads workers to avoid tax by consuming more health insurance and less cash wages. Similarly, individuals can avoid the income tax by spending their income on items that are tax deductible, such as mortgage interest, rather than on items that are not, such as rent. The tax code affects decisions of whether to rent or own a home, whether to live in a state with high or low taxes, whether to donate to charity, and whether to drive a hybrid or conventional fuel car, just to name a few.

Policies that are intended to benefit specific types of taxpayers or activities are known as "tax expenditures" because they are comparable to direct government spending programs. In this chapter, we focus primarily on the effects of the largest tax expenditures for individuals. At the end of the chapter, we address several other issues related to the individual income tax: phase-outs, effective marginal tax rates, and the alternative minimum tax.

UNDERSTANDING TAX EXPENDITURES

The concept of tax expenditures was introduced in the late 1960s to describe the extent to which the tax code strayed from a baseline policy of taxing income on a neutral basis. The purpose of identifying tax expenditures is to highlight when these types of provisions detract from the goal of making the tax system equitable and efficient. Mandated by the Congressional Budget Act of 1974, the

Treasury Department's Office of Tax Analysis (on behalf of the Office of Management and Budget) produces annual estimates of tax expenditures for inclusion in the president's budget, and the Joint Committee on Taxation (on behalf of the Congressional Budget Office) provides its own annual estimates for congressional consideration during legislative decision making.

There are two broad types of tax expenditures: tax credits and tax deductions/exclusions. Preferential tax rates for certain income are a third type of tax expenditure. In 2008, tax credits made up only 19 percent of total tax expenditures, while deductions and exclusions accounted for the remaining 81 percent.

Tax Credits. As we noted in chapter 3, a tax credit is applied after an individual's tax is computed and does not affect the individual's tax rate. A nonrefundable credit (for example, a $1,500 tax credit for the purchase of energy-efficient windows) is applied up to the amount of a taxpayer's tax liability, which means that if the credit is more than the amount of tax owed, the taxpayer does not receive the excess credit. In contrast, a refundable tax credit provides a subsidy to a taxpayer regardless of tax liability, so an individual eligible for a refundable credit receives a check from the Treasury Department for any amount of the credit above what the individual owes in tax. Refundable tax credits are the only type of tax expenditure intended mainly for low- and moderate-income earners, particularly benefiting the bottom

40 percent of taxpayers.

Tax Exclusions/Deductions. Tax exclusions exempt certain items from taxable income, while tax deductions reduce taxable income. As we noted in chapter 3, both types of tax expenditures are applied before the tax is determined. They therefore provide no benefit to those who do not pay income tax. The value of a tax deduction is a function of an individual's marginal tax rate, which means that a tax deduction generally reduces tax liability more for a high-income taxpayer than a low-income taxpayer. Consider, for example, the deduction of charitable contributions. For a high-income taxpayer in the 35 percent bracket, deducting a $100 charitable contribution lowers the taxpayer's tax liability by $35, whereas a low-income taxpayer in the 15 percent bracket receives only a $15 benefit for the same $100 contribution.

STANDARD DEDUCTION AND PERSONAL EXEMPTION

Itemized deductions (e.g., medical care, mortgage interest, certain other taxes, charitable contributions, and casualty losses) are considered tax expenditures, but the standard deduction and personal exemption introduced in chapter 3 are not. Every taxpayer is entitled to take the standard deduction, but taxpayers are permitted to instead itemize allowable deductions, which is desirable if the sum of itemized deductions exceeds the amount of the standard deduction. Despite this option, about two-thirds of all taxpayers claim the standard deduction in a given year. Taxpayers who claim the standard deduction cannot claim their itemized deductions, but are allowed to claim a few other deductions—known as above-the-line deductions—including certain moving expenses and alimony payments.

Some tax reform proposals include a larger standard deduction to simplify the tax code and reduce the number of low-income filers owing federal income tax. Increasing the standard deduction would simplify the tax code for some households and mitigate the increase in tax burden resulting from scaling back or eliminating other tax expenditures. The type of reform we advocate in chapter 6, however, is more fundamental than simply altering existing components of the income tax.

TOP TAX EXPENDITURES

The Joint Committee on Taxation lists nearly two hundred individual income tax expenditures for 2010. Estimates for these tax expenditures total roughly $953 billion. To put this in context, in 2010 the U.S. government collected $2.2 trillion in individual income taxes. If the federal government eliminated individual income tax expenditures—particularly the largest few—marginal tax rates could be reduced drastically across the board without loss of revenue.

The six policy categories with the highest tax expenditure estimates in 2010 were commerce and housing ($288 billion); income security ($208 billion);

TABLE 3. INDIVIDUAL TAX EXPENDITURES BY BUDGET FUNCTION, 2010

BUDGET FUNCTION	NUMBER OF EXPENDITURES	ESTIMATE *in billions*
National Defense	4	$5.8
International Affairs	3	$7.8
General Science, Space, and Technology	3	$0.3
Energy	28	$3.3
Natural Resources and Environment	8	$0.5
Agriculture	7	$0.2
Commerce and Housing		
Housing	13	$137.3
Other business and commerce	28	$126.5
Insurance companies	1	$25.4
Transportation	5	$5.1
Community and Regional Development	12	$3.7
Education, Training, Employment, and Social Services		
Education and training	18	$25.4
Employment	10	$39.1
Social services	7	$88.3
Health	13	$139.2
Medicare	3	$54.6
Income Security	18	$238.8
Social Security and Railroad Retirement	1	$26.8
Veterans' Benefits and Services	4	$5.5
General Purpose Fiscal Assistance	2	$50
Interest	1	$1.3
Total	**192**	**$952.8**

Source: Joint Committee on Taxation, *Estimates of Federal Tax Expenditures for Fiscal Years 2010–2014* (JCS-3-10), December 15, 2010, Table 1.

education, training, employment, and social services ($153 billion); health ($139 billion); Medicare ($55 billion); and general purpose fiscal assistance ($50 billion). The estimates for nearly all of the other categories are quite small in comparison to these top six. In fact, all the other categories combined total only $60

TABLE 4. TOP TEN INDIVIDUAL TAX EXPENDITURES, 2010

EXPENDITURES	ESTIMATE in billions
Exclusion of employer contributions for health care, health insurance premiums, and long-term care insurance premiums	$105.7
Deduction for mortgage interest on owner-occupied residences	$90.8
Reduced rates of tax on dividends and long-term capital gains	$77.7
Making Work Pay credit	$59.7
Earned income credit	$56.2
Credit for children under age 17	$55.1
Defined benefit plans	$38.9
Defined contribution plans	$32.5
Deduction of nonbusiness state and local government income taxes, sales taxes, and personal property taxes	$30.7
Deduction for charitable contributions, other than for education and health	$29.2
Total	$576.5

Source: Joint Committee on Taxation, Estimates of Federal Tax Expenditures for Fiscal Years 2010–2014 (JCS-3-10), December 15, 2010, Table 1..

billion (see table 3).

In 2010, just ten tax expenditures accounted for $577 billion (over 60 percent) of the $953 billion total (see table 4). Three refundable credits, three exclusions, three deductions, and one reduced rate make up the top ten expenditures. Brief descriptions of these follow to illustrate how tax expenditures work and the way they are targeted.

Health. The top tax expenditure in 2010 was the exclusion of employer-provided health insurance. This provision allows employees to exclude the amount their employers pay for their health insurance coverage, as well as their share of the premium, from federal income and payroll taxes. The tax expenditure has been highly criticized by some, both for leading to over-taxation of health care services and for its minimal effect on low-income taxpayers, who often cannot afford employer-sponsored health insurance and, even if they are covered, do not receive less benefit from the subsidy because of their tax law rates. Recent attempts to directly limit the tax expenditure by capping the benefit per taxpayer were rejected in the March 2010 health care reform law. Congress did impose an excise tax, not effective until 2018, on generous (i.e., expensive) health insurance plans. As mentioned above, the exclusion creates excess burden by prompting workers and employers to agree on compensation being provided through health insurance rather than cash wages.

Housing. In the United States, housing is perhaps the least-taxed investment. The primary tax policy related to housing, and the second largest tax expenditure, is the deductibility of home mortgage interest. This tax expenditure imposes excess burden by encouraging those who would otherwise choose to rent to buy a home, or encouraging those who would buy a small home to buy a bigger one due to the tax preference for the interest payments relative to other forms of consumption. Nearly thirty-nine million taxpayers took advantage of this tax expenditure in 2008. Tens of millions more taxpayers have claimed this deduction or will claim it at some point in their lives. Because it is a deduction rather than a credit, the value of this policy rises as one's marginal tax rate rises, making it most beneficial to high-income taxpayers. Therefore, it is not well targeted to encourage homeownership among middle-class households.

Dividends and Capital Gains. The third largest tax expenditure in 2010, and the only preferential rate in the top ten, is the reduced tax rate on dividends and long-term capital gains. A temporarily low tax rate of 15 percent was set in 2003 under the tax cuts initiated by George W. Bush. Originally scheduled to expire at the end of 2008, then extended to the end of 2010, the lower rates are now scheduled to be in effect through the end of 2012. If the tax cuts expire, long-term capital gains will still benefit from a lower rate, but 20 percent rather than 15 percent, and dividends would no longer have a lower tax rate at all, facing tax at each taxpayer's ordinary income tax rate.

It is not clear that these provisions create excess burden. In fact, they are likely to reduce excess burden by diminishing the income tax's penalty on saving, which was discussed in chapter 2.

Refundable Tax Credits. The fourth, fifth, and sixth top tax expenditures in 2010 were refundable tax credits— namely, the Making Work Pay tax credit, the earned income tax credit (EITC), and the child tax credit. All three refundable tax credits phase out as incomes rise, as discussed further below.

The Making Work Pay tax credit was a temporary provision of the American Recovery and Reinvestment Act of 2009. The credit was worth as much as $400 for individual workers and $800 for married couples, subject to income caps. A major campaign initiative from President Obama, it expired at the end of 2010.

The EITC, established in 1975, is targeted at low-income workers. For example, in 2011, those with incomes from work less than $36,052 ($41,132 for married couples filing jointly) with one qualifying child can claim the EITC. The maximum credit is $3,094, available to taxpayers with incomes between $9,100 and $16,690 (between $9,100 and $21,770 for married couples). Both the income cutoff and the amount of the credit increase for those with two children, and both go up an additional amount for those with three or more children. The credit is much more limited for the childless. Nearly twenty-five million people claimed the EITC in 2008.

The child tax credit, established in 1997 at $500 and expanded to $1,000 in 2001 legislation, was claimed by more than twenty-five million taxpayers and is generally available to any taxpayer with a dependent less than seventeen years of age if their modified adjusted gross income is less than $55,000 (single) or $110,000 (married). Assuming that this tax break has little or no effect on people's decision to have children, the excess burden it imposes is likely close to zero.

Retirement Savings. The seventh and eighth largest tax expenditures serve to reduce the tax on savings and investment by excluding net contributions to, and earnings from, retirement plans called defined benefit and defined contribution plans. Though the Joint Committee on Taxation lists these tax expenditures as exclusions, they are actually tax deferrals, because individuals are required to pay tax when they withdraw funds from retirement accounts (except for Roth accounts, which are pretaxed).

With a defined benefit plan, an employer pays a pension, a fixed amount, to employees in their retirement. With a defined contribution plan, usually a 401(k), an employer pays a certain amount annually into a retirement account for an employee, often matching the employee's own contribution. There is no employer-guaranteed amount paid to employees in retirement under defined contribution plans. Instead, an individual's retirement income depends on the accumulations within their 401(k).

As with the lower tax rates for capital gains and dividends, these provisions may reduce excess burden by diminishing the income tax's penalty on saving. But they do not offer an ideal way to achieve this goal. The accounts are clearly a significant source of complexity. There are now more than twenty types of tax-preferred accounts, with each type of account subject to different contribution limits, eligibility rules, and restrictions on withdrawals. Also, taxpayers can obtain tax benefits by shifting money from taxable to tax-free accounts without doing additional saving. Moreover, there is no marginal incentive to save for households that reach the maximum contribution limits.

State and Local Taxes. The ninth largest tax expenditure allows taxpayers to claim as an itemized deduction all nonbusiness state and local government income taxes, sales taxes, and personal property taxes. The appropriateness of this tax expenditure has been questioned because it is a tax subsidy for state taxes, which only further encourages more taxation. The fairness of this tax expenditure is sometimes questioned because some, but not all, taxpayers who receive the subsidy also benefit from state and local services paid for by these taxes. The deduction may create excess burden by prompting taxpayers to move to high-tax states or to vote for higher state taxes and services.

Charitable Giving. The tenth tax expenditure, the deduction for charitable contributions, is also the subject of much debate. Although it is a subsidy for a particular activity, it may not create excess burden, because the activity of charitable giving may provide benefits to third parties. A recent tax proposal contained in President Obama's budget would limit the benefit of all itemized deductions for high-income households to 28 percent, which would somewhat reduce the value of the mortgage interest deduction, state and local tax deductions, and charitable giving deductions for high-income tax dividends.

MARGINAL AND AVERAGE TAX RATES

An important concept for understanding the effects of income taxes that we did not discuss with the soda tax example is marginal tax rates. The excess burden depends on the marginal tax rate, which is the fraction of each additional dollar of income that is absorbed by tax, rather than the average tax rate. Again, the excess burden arises because taxpayers change their behavior in order to avoid the tax. Their incentive to do this depends on the amount by which their tax liability changes when they change their behavior, not on the total amount that they already pay. When a person decides whether additional work is "worth it," she looks at the extra wages she will earn from that work minus the *extra taxes she will pay on those wages*, not her total taxes.

For example, suppose that the tax system allows a $50,000 exemption and applies a flat 20 percent tax on taxable income above that amount. A taxpayer with $100,000 income owes $10,000 tax, so her average tax rate is a mere 10 percent. But her incentive to change her behavior depends on her 20 percent marginal tax rate. When deciding whether another dollar of taxable income is worth earning, she should look at whether the sacrifices involved in earning that income are greater than or less than 80 cents, because that is the fraction of the additional dollar that she will be allowed to keep. The fact that the first $50,000 of her income is tax exempt, which makes her average tax rate only 10 percent, is irrelevant to the decision of whether to earn another dollar, because the new dollar is subject to the 20 percent marginal tax rate.

Providing the $50,000 exemption makes the tax system less burdensome on low-income taxpayers, but tends to increase the excess burden relative to tax revenue. The taxpayer faces the same marginal tax rate as she would under a 20 percent flat-rate tax with no exemption, resulting in the same excess burden, but the tax raises significantly less revenue than a 20 percent flat tax.

If the tax system is already progressive, efforts to

make it more progressive can have high excess burden. For example, consider a proposal to increase taxes by 5 percent of the income above $250,000. The resulting revenue is less than 5 percent of the affected taxpayers' incomes because the tax applies only to the income above the $250,000 threshold; for example, for a couple earning $400,000, the 5-percentage-point tax increase applies only to the last $150,000 of taxable income, and the revenue is only $7,500. Because the disincentive effects depend on the marginal tax rate applied to the last dollar, though, they are as severe as if the couple had to pay an extra 5 percent on their entire income (except that the disincentive will not prompt the taxpayer to reduce her taxable income below $250,000).

The opposite pattern holds for tax hikes in the bottom bracket, which actually leave marginal rates unchanged for most of the taxpayers from whom additional revenue is collected. For example, suppose that the 10 percent bracket, which applies to the first $17,000 of a couple's taxable income in 2011, was increased to 15 percent. Taxpayers in that bracket would face a 5-percentage-point increase in disincentives and would pay an additional 5 percent of taxable income. At the same time, all couples in higher brackets would also pay an additional $850 in tax, because the first $17,000 of their income would be taxed at 15 rather than 10 percent. Although additional revenues would be collected from these higher-bracket taxpayers, they would not face any additional disincentives, because there would be no change in their marginal last-dollar tax rate.

In this discussion, we have assumed that the marginal tax rate is equal to the taxpayer's bracket. Things are not that simple, though, because income-based phase-outs also alter the effective marginal tax rates that taxpayers face.

PHASE-OUTS AND EFFECTIVE MARGINAL TAX RATES

As we mentioned above, many tax expenditures in the U.S. tax system are limited for taxpayers as their incomes rise. In other words, these tax breaks phase out as incomes rise. Income-based phase-outs raise the tax payments of higher-income taxpayers and can thereby promote progressivity. However, they are also a source of excess burden—increasing effective marginal tax rates (EMTRs), which result in a disincentive to work and earn income. The EMTR, the change in tax liability that occurs when an additional dollar of income is earned, measures the impact of the tax system on the incentive to earn income.

For example, when a credit is phased out, the marginal rate is increased by the phase-out rate; if a $100 income increase causes a taxpayer to lose $3 of a credit, the EMTR rises by 3 percentage points. When a deduction or exclusion is phased out, the marginal rate is increased by the statutory rate multiplied by the phase-out rate; if a $100 income increase causes a taxpayer to lose $10 of a deduction, and the taxpayer is in the 35 percent bracket, the resulting increase in tax payments is \$3.50, and the EMTR rises by 3.5 percentage points. Even if taxpayers do not respond to specific phase-outs with reduced incentive to earn more income, they may be deterred from earning income by the general awareness that phase-outs exist.

THE BIG PICTURE: THE SENSITIVITY OF TAXABLE INCOME TO TAX RATES

It is very difficult to track each of the ways in which individuals can change their behavior to avoid the income tax. Fortunately, there is no need to do so. The basic determinant of the amount of excess burden is the overall change in individuals' behavior to avoid the income tax. As Seth H. Giertz observed in a recent analysis, estimates from statistical studies have generally found that taxable income displays significant sensitivity to marginal tax rates, at least for high-income households.

SHRINKING INCOME TAX ROLLS

When the income tax was first introduced, it targeted only the very wealthy, affecting less than 1 percent of Americans. Legislation in the 1940s broadened its reach. Over the years, the percentage of households paying income tax has fluctuated. In 2009, only 53 percent of households paid individual income tax. Nearly half of the population did not pay individual income tax, either because their income was offset by exemptions and deductions or because their tax liability was offset by credits.

For example, in 2011, a typical married couple with two children would have zero individual income tax liability if their income was $45,776 and would actually have negative individual income tax liability (receiving cash from refundable credits) if their income was below this amount. At an income of $45,776, the couple would claim four personal exemptions totaling $14,800 ($3,700 each) and a standard deduction of $11,600, leaving a taxable income of $19,376. On this income, the couple would initially owe tax of $2,056 (10 percent of $17,000 plus 15 percent of $2,376). But this tax liability would be wiped out by $2,000 of child tax credits ($1,000 per child) and a $56 earned income tax credit.

One argument against allowing a large number of households to pay no federal income tax is that those without a vested interest in the tax system will be indifferent about federal spending. Owing no federal income tax can seriously diminish concern for the size and efficiency of government. A high number of nontaxable returns could make constraining the size of government more difficult.

SUMMARY

The tax code is fraught with tax expenditures intended to benefit certain taxpayers or their activities. In 2010, tax expenditures geared toward individuals totaled $953 billion, with just ten tax expenditures making up more than 60 percent of this amount. Many tax expenditures phase out as incomes rise. These subsidies often give rise to excess burden by inducing taxpayers to change their behavior.

5

ISSUES IN U.S. BUSINESS TAXATION

The tax treatment of business activity depends on the business's organizational form. A C corporation, a separate legal entity owned by holders of transferable stock certificates who have limited liability for the corporation's actions, is subject to the corporate income tax, like an individual is. C corporations (so called because they are taxed under subchapter C of chapter 1 of the tax code) are generally the largest firms in the economy. Alternatively, noncorporate businesses organized as partnerships, sole proprietorships, and S corporations (taxed under subchapter S instead of subchapter C and differing from C corporations in ways discussed below) are considered "pass-through" entities for tax purposes. These tend to be smaller businesses than C corporations. The income of businesses that qualify as pass-through entities is taxed only as personal income to their shareholders or partners.

In the first part of this chapter, we will focus on current business tax law as it relates to both C corporations and pass-through entities. In the second part, we will address issues arising in business taxation and discuss the controversy surrounding the corporate income tax.

STRUCTURAL COMPONENTS OF BUSINESS TAXATION
As mentioned in chapter 3, the tax base for a business is its total revenue minus wages paid to employees, interest payments on loans, and depreciation of assets. Foreign as well as domestic income is included in the tax base, but multinational corporations receive a credit for taxes

paid in other countries. Tax on foreign-source income is also generally deferred until the income is repatriated to—that is, brought back into—the United States. A similarity to the individual income tax is the existence of a corporate alternative minimum tax, which is parallel to the regular tax.

Taxation of business income differs from that of individual income in that the only allowable deductions are related to business expenses. Dividends paid to stockholders, however, are not considered business expenses and are therefore not deductible, which means that individual stockholders of C corporations pay tax on dividends already taxed under the corporate income tax (discussed further below). Because pass-through businesses do not pay corporate income tax, an important distinction between corporate and pass-through business taxes is that corporate income is taxed twice.

The structure of business taxation seems fairly straightforward, but in reality it is complicated because of the technical nature of calculating depreciation (discussed further below) and the complex rules governing acquisitions and foreign income, as well as different treatment for the mineral industries, financial institutions, and tax-exempt organizations.

CORPORATE INCOME TAX RATES

Because pass-through entities are not taxed under the corporate income tax, this discussion of tax rates applies only to C corporations. For these corporations, the statutory tax rate for income is generally considered a flat rate because most income is earned by firms that are large enough to be taxed at the highest rate (35 percent).

As mentioned in chapter 3, the top corporate income tax rate has historically been very high, peaking at 52.8 percent in 1968–69 and only dropping to 46 percent by the late 1970s. The Tax Reform Act of 1986 lowered the highest rate from 46 percent to 34 percent. This rate was raised one point in 1993 and has remained at 35 percent ever since. The *effective* marginal tax rate, however, differs from this statutory rate because different assets are taxed differently due to the tax code's failure to accurately, or even consistently, measure asset depreciation.

ASSET DEPRECIATION

Depreciation rules are an important component for determining the effective tax rate on capital income. Though companies are allowed to deduct the cost of doing business from their income, there is a problem aligning the cost of long-term assets with income earned because the expense and receipt of income often do not occur simultaneously. The concept of depreciation addresses this issue. Tax depreciation describes the rate at which businesses are allowed to deduct the cost of capital investment over a period of time.

Calculating deductions such as interest paid on loans and wages paid to employees is fairly straightforward, but calculating the cost of a capital investment is usually much trickier. For example, consider a snow removal company that buys a new snowplow. The purchase is a one-time event, but the snowplow will generate revenue for the company beyond the year in which it is purchased. Instead of deducting the entire amount immediately, the company spreads the deduction over the period of years allowed by the depreciation schedule.

Depreciation schedules often differ from true economic depreciation (the asset's actual life span). In some cases, tax depreciation schedules are too long, but many times they are too short relative to economic depreciation. This mismatch between economic depreciation and existing tax depreciation schedules is often intentional. Accelerated depreciation—allowing faster write-offs than actual economic depreciation—is considered a policy tool to stimulate investment. However, targeted preferences for certain asset classes result in distortions in investment decisions.

Depreciation schedules are not the only instances of preferential treatment in business taxation. Just as different asset types face different effective tax rates, different financing structures underlying investments—namely, debt or equity financing—are also taxed differently, leading to distortions in investment financing and excess burden.

DEBT VERSUS EQUITY FINANCING

Debt financing occurs when a business takes out a loan, and equity financing occurs when a firm raises capital by selling stock in the business. In the current tax system, excess burden arises because debt financing is tax-favored relative to equity financing. This is so because firms are allowed to deduct interest costs from their income, whereas they are not allowed to deduct dividends paid to shareholders. Dividends are, in effect, the cost of using shareholders' funds, just as interest is the cost of using a financial institution's funds. This makes investments that are financed through debt issuance subject to less tax liability than equity-financed investments.

For example, if the tax rate is 35 percent, and a company pays $100 in interest, the company deducts that $100 from its income, thereby saving $35 in taxes and lowering the net cost of the interest payment to $65. Because no equivalent deduction is afforded a company that finances an investment with equity, debt-financed investments incur less tax and face a lower effective tax rate than equity-financed investments. A disparity still exists even after accounting for the favorable individual income tax treatment of dividends discussed in chapter 3. This state of affairs is problematic because it encourages businesses to take greater risks by choosing debt-financed investment over more stable equity financing.

INTERNATIONAL ISSUES

The U.S. tax code taxes income on a worldwide basis, which means that income a U.S. company earns outside of the United States is subject to taxation. This foreign-source income is awarded a tax credit of the value of foreign income tax paid abroad, and any remaining tax is due to the Treasury Department at the time that income is repatriated to the United States. However, complex rules prevent some companies from claiming full credit for taxes paid overseas.

Taxation on a worldwide basis is not common among U.S. trading partners. Most other developed countries, including Canada, France, Germany, and the Netherlands, operate under what is known as a territorial tax system. Under this type of system, only active income earned domestically is taxed—foreign-source active income is not taxed at all. (Passive income, such as interest income, is generally taxed on a worldwide basis.) According to the Treasury Department, U.S. taxation of foreign-source income outstrips every other country in breadth and complexity.

As we discussed in chapter 3, the top U.S. corporate tax rate is also significantly higher than that in most other developed countries, which provides a disincentive for U.S. multinational companies to repatriate income to the United States.

To make this clearer, suppose that a U.S. corporation earns $1,000 in a country with a 20 percent corporate income tax. The U.S. company would pay $200 in tax to that country. When the corporation repatriated the income to the United States, it would owe $350 in taxes at the 35 percent tax rate but would receive a $200 tax credit for the foreign tax already paid and thus would owe only $150. However, a U.S. corporation can face a penalty when compared with a foreign competitor who faces no additional tax because its home country has a territorial tax system. The U.S. system gives rise to excess burden because the U.S.-based corporation has a disincentive to repatriate earnings and thereby is at a competitive disadvantage relative to a corporation based abroad that does not face the additional U.S. tax burden.

If the U.S. statutory rate was less than or equal to that of the host country where the foreign source income was earned, the foreign tax credit would eliminate any U.S. tax liability and create a level playing field for the U.S.-based multinational corporation.

SECTOR-SPECIFIC ISSUES

One reason that the corporate tax code is complex is that it includes multiple industry-specific policies. For example, energy-related tax policies are numerous. In 2010, corporate tax expenditures targeting the energy sector totaled more than $5 billion. The fossil fuel sector has generally been tax-favored, with various production and investment tax credits available to companies. The Energy Policy Act of 2005 also created a number of new provisions in the corporate income tax that favor energy efficiency.

Another example of sector-specific tax policies is in the realm of financial institutions. Savings banks and savings and loan associations (known as thrift institutions), commercial banks, and insurance companies are all generally subject to the corporate income tax. But thrift institutions and commercial banks receive preferential tax treatment in that they are allowed to deduct funds they set aside in reserve in case they need to cover bad debts. Similarly, insurance companies are allowed to deduct certain amounts set aside for future costs. Credit unions, many of which operate like large banks, are exempt from income tax entirely. Excess burden occurs when the tax system favors investment in some industries over others.

PASS-THROUGH ENTITIES

S corporations are the most prevalent form of pass-through entity. And since 1997, S corporations have also been the most common corporate entity. (A corporate entity can claim S corporation status if it has less than one hundred shareholders and only one stock class, among other requirements.) In 2010, the IRS counted 4.5 million S corporations and only 2.4 million C corporations, while partnerships totaled 3.5 million. The growth of S corporations has been rapid; in 1980 there were only half a million of these entities.

Smaller businesses are tax-favored in other ways as well. For example, under section 179 of the Internal Revenue Code, small firms receive more generous tax treatment on equipment and software investments, with a large immediate deduction. For bigger firms, however, the amount that can be immediately deducted is subject to certain limitations before the provision phases out entirely.

CORPORATE INCOME TAX CONTROVERSY

Most tax experts agree that some form of corporate tax is necessary to prevent individuals from avoiding the individual income tax by sheltering money in companies, but the current system is highly criticized by academics, policymakers, and practitioners alike. One reason for criticism is, as mentioned above, the taxation of dividends in the individual income tax as well as the corporate income tax, which amounts to double taxation. Some analysts also argue that the corporate income tax reduces and distorts business investment.

The main controversy over the corporate income tax reflects the uncertainty over the incidence of the tax, that is, who is worse off because the tax is paid. Economic incidence describes who actually bears the burden of the tax, while statutory incidence indicates who is legally responsible for paying the tax. Although corporations are legally responsible for paying the corporate income tax, only individuals can bear the economic burden. There is some argument, however, over who bears the burden—stockholders, consumers (through higher prices), or employees (through lower wages)— and in what proportion. This is complicated by the fact that where incidence falls in the short term can shift in the long run.

SUMMARY

There are two general categories for businesses that determine how they are taxed: C corporations, which are subject to a corporate income tax, and pass-through entities, whose income is taxed as shareholders' or partners' personal income. This system results in double taxation for shareholders of C corporations, because they are taxed as individuals on dividends after the C corporation has already paid income tax. In addition, there is controversy over who bears the incidence of the corporate income tax—shareholders, workers, or consumers.

Another departure from neutrality in business taxation is asset depreciation, given the general difficulty of aligning the cost of long-term assets with income earned, as well as the artificially short depreciation schedules policymakers assign to certain assets in order to affect business behavior. Yet another departure from neutrality is the tax treatment of financing options. Interest on business loans is deductible, whereas dividends paid to shareholders is not, effectively favoring debt financing over equity financing.

Finally, the United States taxes U.S. companies on a worldwide basis and also has a much higher corporate tax rate than other developed countries. This combination serves as a disincentive for U.S. corporations to repatriate income to the United States.

As discussed in chapter 2, any income tax introduces excess burden, because it taxes saving and investment more heavily than current consumption. But the actual U.S. business income tax system causes even more excess burden by taxing some forms of investment more heavily than other forms.

6

**OPTIONS FOR
FUNDAMENTAL
TAX REFORM**

The preceding chapters describe some of the challenges and problems posed by the current U.S. tax system. While some of these problems can be addressed by improving the income tax, perhaps by eliminating tax preferences and lowering tax rates, that approach leaves the income tax's saving penalty in place.

In this chapter we discuss the possibility of a more fundamental tax reform, involving a movement toward consumption taxation. We explained the motivation for such a reform in chapter 2. Income taxes, no matter how well designed, create excess burden by discouraging saving. In contrast, consumption taxes and wage taxes avoid this problem by treating saving and current consumption neutrally. As we explained in chapter 2, consumption taxes are generally preferable to wage taxes because they raise some revenue from saving without penalizing it.

We therefore consider the prospect of introducing a consumption tax as either a partial or complete replacement for the income tax.

DIFFERENT WAYS TO TAX CONSUMPTION

We begin by discussing the different ways in which consumption can be taxed: the retail sales tax, the value-added tax, the flat tax, the X tax, and the personal expenditures tax.

Retail Sales Tax. A retail sales tax is conceptually the simplest to see as a tax on consumption because, in its pure textbook form, it is imposed only on retail sales to consumers. Sales from one business to another are excluded from the tax base. When they hear the term "consumption tax," many people think of sales taxes. The FairTax plan, developed by Americans for Fair Taxation, proposes to replace the individual and corporate income tax, estate and gift tax, and payroll and self-employment taxes with a national retail sales tax.

Value-Added Tax. A VAT, like a retail sales tax, applies to goods and services sold to consumers and is therefore a tax on consumption. But unlike a retail sales tax, which is collected once, on the final sale to a consumer, a VAT is imposed and collected at every stage in the production and distribution of a good or service. This collection structure helps prevent the tax from being evaded at the retail level, making the tax easier to enforce. Each firm is taxed on its value added, which is its sales to consumers and other firms minus its purchases from other firms. Sales between firms face no net tax, because the seller is taxed while the buyer claims a deduction.

Figure 1 illustrates the relationship of the VAT to the sales tax in an economy with two firms and two individuals. Firm A produces a machine that it sells for $100 to Firm B and pays $70 of wages to Jones, its employee. Firm B buys the machine for $100, pays $40 wages to its employee Smith, and produces $150 of consumer goods. Jones buys $90 of the consumer goods and Smith buys the remaining $60.

FIGURE 1. FOUR WAYS TO TAX CONSUMPTION

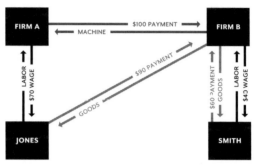

150 TOTAL CONSUMPTION

Retail Sales Tax: B 150   *Flat tax / X tax:* A 30, B 10, JONES 70, SMITH 40
VAT: A 100, B 50   *PET:* JONES 90, SMITH 60

Under a retail sales tax, tax is collected from firm B on the $150 of consumer goods that it sold. Under a VAT, tax is collected from firm A on the sale of the $100 machine and from firm B on its $50 value added ($150 sales to consumers minus $100 machine purchase). Because the sale of the machine washes out, the VAT is equivalent to the sales tax.

Flat Tax and X Tax. In 1983, Robert Hall and Alvin Rabushka proposed the "flat" tax, which is a two-part VAT. Firms compute value added, but deduct their wage payments to compute their business cash flow. Workers are then taxed on their wages. The total tax base is the same as under a VAT and therefore the same as under a retail sales tax.

Because the VAT is a consumption tax and the flat tax is simply a two-part VAT, the flat tax is also a consumption tax. Firms are taxed at a single flat rate— say, 25 percent—on business cash flow, while workers are taxed at that same rate on wages above a substantial exemption amount. Workers with earnings below the exemption amount pay zero tax, those with incomes moderately above the exemption amount pay a small fraction of their wages in tax, and those with very high earnings pay close to 25 percent. That pattern ensures some degree of progressivity across workers. Meanwhile, consumption financed from business cash flow is taxed at the full 25 percent.

The Bradford X tax is a modification of the flat tax. Under the X tax, a set of tax brackets, higher for those with higher wages, is used to make the tax more progressive. The top bracket for those with the highest wages matches the tax rate that firms pay on business cash flow.

Figure 1 shows how the flat tax and X tax work in the simple economy. Firm A is taxed on $30 cash flow ($100 value added minus $70 wage payment), and Firm B is taxed on $10 cash flow ($50 value added minus $40 wage payment). Smith and Jones are taxed on the wages they receive.

Personal Expenditures Tax (PET). The personal expenditures tax, sometimes called a consumed-income tax, takes a completely different approach. Under this tax, each household files an annual tax return on which it reports income, deducts all saving (deposits into savings accounts, asset purchases, amounts lent to others, and payments made on outstanding debts) and adds all dissaving (withdrawals from savings accounts, gross proceeds of asset sales, amounts borrowed from others, and payments received on outstanding loans). The resulting measure equals the household's consumption, which is taxed at progressive rates. As shown in figure 1, each individual is taxed on his or her consumption under the PET.

COMPARISON OF CONSUMPTION TAXES

As the above discussion reveals, the sales tax and the VAT are very similar to each other, differing only in their administrative collection mechanisms. The VAT is administratively more burdensome, because firms that sell to other firms must report these transactions, whereas only sales to consumers need be reported under the sales tax. The sales tax may therefore be preferable at a low tax rate. At a high tax rate, though, the incentive to evade tax becomes greater, which may support the use of a VAT, because it is easier to enforce, as explained above.

A sales tax or VAT is relatively simple because it is collected from firms at a flat tax rate. No effort is made to identify the amounts consumed by specific households or to tax those households at different tax rates. This feature is problematic, though, because taxing all consumers at the same rate is likely to be viewed as burdensome on the poor. This problem can be addressed by providing rebates, but this is a limited measure. Taxing necessities at lower rates than luxuries is another common solution, but leads to complexity and inefficiency.

Because of concerns about its burden on the poor and middle class, a sales tax or VAT would probably not be adopted as a full replacement of the income tax system, in the manner proposed by the FairTax plan. Instead, the tax would probably be adopted as only a partial replacement of the income tax system. Partial replacement of the income tax would offer smaller economic gains than full replacement because it would not fully remove the excess burden caused by the income tax's penalty on saving. Also, having a sales tax or VAT available alongside an income tax could spur government spending.

Full removal of the saving penalty and the associated excess burden requires that the income tax system be completely replaced by a consumption tax. A complete-replacement tax would probably need to be more progressive than the sales tax, VAT, or even the flat tax, requiring the use of an X tax or PET.

Although the PET has not received much interest recently, the X tax got a little attention in 2005. In one of the two tax reform options presented in its report, the President's Advisory Panel on Federal Tax Reform proposed that most of the income tax system be replaced with an X tax, with a top 30 percent tax rate, although the plan called for a 15 percent tax on capital income to be retained. Some members of the panel favored an alternative that would have completely replaced the income tax system with an X tax with a 35 percent top tax rate. Congress did not, however, consider or act upon the panel's recommendations.

The PET and the X tax implement progressive consumption taxation in different ways. The PET achieves finely calibrated progressivity by linking each household's tax rate to its annual consumer spending. To achieve this goal, however, the PET requires a wide range of financial transactions to be reported on household tax returns. The X tax achieves progressivity in a less refined manner, by taxing business cash flow at a high flat rate and taxing households' wages at rates that depend on annual wages rather than annual consumer spending. (The high flat rate on business cash flow promotes progressivity, because this revenue comes from above-normal investment returns and capital already in place before the tax is introduced, both of which tend to accrue to relatively well-off people.) The X tax is simpler than the PET, though, because only wages need be reported on household tax returns.

SUMMARY

A movement toward consumption taxation could be achieved by partially replacing the income tax system with a value-added tax. A more complete movement to consumption taxation could be achieved by replacing the entire income tax system with a progressive consumption tax.

CONCLUSION

In this book, we have argued that excess burden is the real burden of taxation, more than the dollars and cents paid to the government. Excess burden arises whenever taxpayers change their behavior to avoid paying taxes, suffering a loss of freedom with no corresponding revenue gain to the government. Excess burden can be as prosaic as a decision to buy fewer cartons of soda in response to a soda tax or as profound as a decision to save and invest less for the future in response to the income tax. In setting tax policy, our elected representatives must consider many goals, including simplicity and fairness. As they balance these goals, they should also strive to reduce excess burden and thereby promote individual freedom.

SUGGESTED READING

CHAPTER 1: WHAT IS EXCESS BURDEN?

For a more complete and more technical discussion of excess burden, see Harvey S. Rosen and Ted Gayer, *Public Finance*, 9th ed. (New York: McGraw-Hill/Irwin, 2010), 329–51.

CHAPTER 2: EXCESS BURDEN OF WAGE, INCOME, AND CONSUMPTION TAXES

For a more complete and more technical discussion of the excess burden of taxes on work and saving, see Rosen and Gayer, *Public Finance*, 415–32. For an analysis of statistical estimates of how tax rates affect work decisions, see Nada Eissa, "Evidence on Labor Supply and Taxes, and Implications for Tax Policy," in *Tax Policy Lessons from the 2000s*, ed. Alan D. Viard (Washington, D.C.: AEI Press, 2009), 45–91.

CHAPTER 3: TAXATION IN THE UNITED STATES: AN OVERVIEW

For an exhaustive history of the U.S. tax system, see Joseph A. Pechman, *Federal Tax Policy*, 5th ed. (Washington, D.C.: Brookings Institution Press, 1987).

CHAPTER 4: ISSUES IN U.S. PERSONAL INCOME TAXATION

For a survey of the statistical studies on how taxable income responds to marginal tax rates, see Seth H. Giertz, "The Elasticity of Taxable Income: Influences on Economic Efficiency and Tax Revenues, and Implications for Tax Policy," in *Tax Policy Lessons from the 2000s*, ed. Alan D. Viard (Washington, D.C.: AEI Press, 2009), 101–36, available at www.aei.org/book/975. For more on the tax expenditure for charitable giving, see Alex Brill and Philip Swagel, "An Uncharitable Proposal," *The American*, March 26, 2009, available at http://american.com/archive/2009/march-2009/an-uncharitable-proposal.

CHAPTER 5: ISSUES IN U.S. BUSINESS TAXATION

For a thorough understanding of U.S. corporate taxation, see Daniel N. Shaviro, *Decoding the U.S. Corporate Tax* (Washington, D.C.: Urban Institute Press), 2009. For reasons to reduce the corporate income tax rate, see Alex Brill, "Corporate Tax Rates: Receipts and

Distortions," *Tax Notes*, December 22, 2008, available at www.aei.org/
article/29132. For reasons to eliminate the corporate income tax,
see Alan D. Viard, "Three Cheers for the Decline of the Corporate
Income Tax," *Tax Policy Outlook*, April 2008, available at www.aei.org/
outlook/27770. For a discussion of tax policy for large and small
businesses, see Alan D. Viard and Amy Roden, "Big Business: The
Other Engine of Economic Growth," *Tax Policy Outlook*, June 2009,
available at www.aei.org/outlook/100051.

CHAPTER 6: OPTIONS FOR FUNDAMENTAL TAX REFORM

For a discussion of tax reform options and a set of proposals,
see President's Advisory Panel on Federal Tax Reform, "Simple,
Fair, and Pro-Growth: Proposals to Fix America's Tax System,"
November 2005, available through http://govinfo.library.unt.edu/
taxreformpanel/final-report/index.html.

Alex M. Brill is a research fellow at the American Enterprise Institute (AEI). Prior to joining AEI, he was policy director and chief economist to the House Committee on Ways and Means. He also served on the staff of the President's Council of Economic Advisers and as a consultant to the National Commission on Fiscal Responsibility and Reform. In these roles, Mr. Brill worked on a variety of economic and legislative policy issues, including a myriad of tax policy issues.

Alan D. Viard is a resident scholar at the American Enterprise Institute (AEI). Previously, he was a senior economist at the Federal Reserve Bank of Dallas and an assistant professor of economics at Ohio State University. He has also worked for the Treasury Department's Office of Tax Analysis, the President's Council of Economic Advisers, and the Joint Committee on Taxation. Mr. Viard has written on a wide variety of tax and budget issues.